WAYS TO PRAY WITH CHILDREN

WAYS to PRAY with CHILDREN

Prayers, Services, & Activities

Barbara Ann Bretherton

XXIII

TWENTY-THIRD PUBLICATIONS

Mystic, Connecticut 06355

North American Edition 1996

Originally published in 1995 as *Praying with Children* by Social Science Press, Wentworth Falls, NSW, Australia.

Twenty-Third Publications
185 Willow Street
P.O. Box 180
Mystic, CT 06355
(860) 536-2611
(800) 321-0411

ISBN 0-89622-670-0
Library of Congress Catalog Card Number 95-78538
Printed in the U.S.A.

FOREWORD

In religious education we want our students to know and experience something of the richness of our Christian faith tradition. Even more, we want our children to develop a personal relationship with a loving God. Prayer is at the heart of religious education in the school, the parish, and the family.

To pray with children is both a challenge and a privilege. The teaching of prayer requires not only the development of special skills, but also a commitment to prayer on the part of the teacher. Children begin to pray as parents pray with them at particular times of the day such as bedtime and mealtime. Similarly, prayer is taught in a school or religious education class when the teacher engages the students *in* prayer. Religious education classes also teach *about* prayer by explaining its place in our faith tradition, its many forms, and its importance in building a relationship with God.

Ways to Pray with Children: Prayers, Activities, and Services, by Barbara Bretherton, makes a valuable contribution to this crucial area. It provides both a source of knowledge about prayer as well as a wealth of creative and practical activities to assist teachers as they lead children into prayer. The various aspects of prayer which are considered are comprehensive and range from simple prayer suggestions to carefully prepared prayer services. The clear layout of the book makes it very "user friendly."

As a parent, catechist, and classroom teacher, I find the prayer suggestions and activities to be a source of both practical assistance and personal inspiration. Teachers, catechists, and parents are fortunate to be able to draw upon the wealth of professional experience, creativity, and personal commitment to prayer which is represented in this wonderful resource.

Begin to use this resource today!

Dr. Marie MacDonald
Head of Department, Religious Education (Victoria)
Australian Catholic University

ACKNOWLEDGMENTS

This book could not have been completed without the support of colleagues and friends.

I wish in particular to express my sincere thanks to Barbara Fyfe for her constant and careful reading of the text, her assistance with the layout, and for her advice and encouragement throughout the preparation of the work.

I am also indebted to Jenny O'Brien for the computerization of the music contained in the text. Finally, I wish to acknowledge the ongoing contribution of creative, dedicated, and faith-filled teachers with whom I have worked and who are a constant inspiration and source of ideas for all religious educators.

CONTENTS

WAYS TO PRAY WITH CHILDREN

INTRODUCTION

Teach children to pray and you have given them a most precious gift for life.

Prayer connects us with God. It puts us in touch with the very source of our being, the God who not only created us but who loves us, communicates with us, and walks the journey of life with us as our invisible friend.

Prayer connects us with each other. It brings us together to express our faith in an all-knowing, all-loving, all-wise God who reveals to us the meaning of life's mysteries and who shows us how to care for each other, to live together in harmony, and to care for the earth.

Prayer is our lifeline to the God of goodness, beauty, and truth, the God who both comforts us and challenges us in our Christian living.

Prayer is an essential element of the religious education of children. Through prayer, children are able to express and deepen their relationship with God. It is the task of the religion teacher to assist students in the development of their prayer life.

Ways to Pray with Children is a "how to" resource book designed to facilitate the teaching and practice of prayer and to encourage an attitude of prayerfulness in children. The text provides teachers with numerous and comprehensive examples of the many elements that can contribute to prayer in the lives of primary students. It recognizes the need for teachers to make prayer practical, enjoyable, easily accessible, and relevant to the lives of today's children.

Ways to Pray with Children presents a variety of new ideas, encompassing many different prayer forms. Teachers will find the text easy to read and the instructions easy to follow.

The aim of *Ways to Pray with Children* is to assist and support teachers of religion in their privileged task of enabling children to build and deepen their relationship with God through prayer.

WHAT IS PRAYER?

PRAYER IS:

COMMUNICATING WITH GOD

KEEPING GOD COMPANY

TUNING INTO GOD

TALKING WITH MY GODFRIEND

LOVING GOD

PRAYER IS THE MEANS BY WHICH WE EXPRESS OUR RELATIONSHIP WITH GOD.

BEING IN GOD'S PRESENCE

WAITING ON GOD

LISTENING TO GOD

LOOKING AT GOD

DANCING FOR GOD

PRAYER IS OUR RESPONSE TO A LOVING AND COMPASSIONATE GOD WHO IS
CONSTANTLY CALLING US AND WHO IS ALWAYS THERE FOR US.

CREATING THE ENVIRONMENT FOR PRAYER

We cannot make children pray, but we can create an environment that encourages prayer. Prayerful images, soft music, dimmed lighting, comfortable posture, and an atmosphere of peacefulness and quiet all assist in helping children to pray. Young children respond to and need concrete images to assist them in the development of a prayer life in the same way that concrete materials help them to learn other educational concepts and skills.

A SPECIAL PLACE

Develop a prayer corner in a prominent place in the classroom to provide a focus for prayer and a constant reminder of the presence and closeness of God.

THE PRAYER TABLE

Establish a prayer table within the prayer corner.

THE TABLE COVER

Collect or make a series of tablecloths with which to cover the table. The following suggestion has been used successfully.

Prepare a different colored cloth for each of the liturgical seasons of the year.

Purple: Advent and Lent

White: Christmas, Easter, and all major feast days of Jesus and Mary

Gold: Easter (for "extra" celebratory emphasis)

Red: Pentecost, Good Friday, and the feasts of martyrs

Green: Ordinary time (a time—between Pentecost and the new season of Advent—for growing and developing in the faith)

Use the different colors at the beginning of each new season to highlight the mood and focus of the praying church—the family of God at prayer.

PRAYER CLOTH OR PRAYER MAT

Hem a piece of plain white cloth. Allow the children to write their names on it or draw a picture or symbol of themselves on it (e.g., a hand trace or print). Decorate or color the cloth appropriately and use this to "dress" the prayer table at the beginning of the year and for special occasions and feast days.

NOTE: These cloths may also be placed on the floor to form part of a centerpiece for prayer—a focus around which the teacher and children may gather.

THE BIBLE

Introduce the Bible to your prayer table. The Word of God may be given prominence on the prayer table by sometimes celebrating it with a welcome procession (e.g., a child might hold up the Bible and carry it to the prayer table accompanied by candle bearers and the singing of a hymn or antiphon).

❏   It is important to elevate the Bible on a bookstand.

❏   Use the introduction to the gospels used at Mass when you are having a formal reading from the gospels in class (e.g., during a prayer service or paraliturgy).

❏   Have the children prepare to listen to the Word of God by signing their forehead, lips, and heart and saying a prayer such as, "May your words Jesus/God be in my mind, on my lips, and in my heart."

❏   Wear a prayer shawl occasionally for reading the Word of God, especially the gospels.

❏   Ensure you have a suitable children's Bible available for the children to read and/or look at.

THE CANDLE

Place a candle on the prayer table or prayer mat. Light this candle whenever you pray with the children as a sign of the ongoing presence of the risen Jesus in their midst. Decorated, aromatic, and colorful candles from retail stores are useful.

A paschal candle for the season of Easter creates a link between parish liturgy and school prayer.

❏   Celebrate Candlemas Day (February 2nd).

Arrange to have classroom candles blessed and distributed at a special school paraliturgy on February 2nd, the Feast of the Presentation of Jesus in the Temple. This feast day is traditionally the day when the Catholic Church blesses candles for use throughout the year. The Gospel of the day (Lk 2:22–40) tells the story of Mary and Joseph taking the infant Jesus to the temple for consecration to the Lord. There the holy man Simeon proclaims Jesus as the light that will save the world.

(A suggested format for a prayer service or paraliturgy is provided in the chapter "Prayer Services/Paraliturgies.")

❏   For extra symbolism, make your own class candle.

Instructions:

• Encourage children to bring to school a small piece of candle from home (perhaps a birthday candle).

• Purchase some paraffin wax from the local supermarket.

• Melt the children's candle pieces and some of the paraffin in a saucepan.

• Pour the multicolored wax into a cut-down milk carton and add a piece of white string for the wick.

• When firm, cut away the cardboard carton.

The resulting multicolored class candle is a powerful reminder of the presence of Jesus in each person and of the unity of the class members—one with Jesus and one with one another in faith and love.

THE DECOR

Consider keeping some fresh flowers, a growing plant, or some greenery on the table as a gift to God—a reminder of God's beautiful world and of the gift of creation. Encourage the children to be responsible for keeping the prayer table attractive. This helps to create a sense of ownership on their part and the action itself becomes a prayer.

OTHER ARTIFACTS AND SYMBOLS

❏   Collect a variety of objects which may provide a focus for prayer at different times. Some examples are:

- sacred images—crucifix, statue, picture of Jesus or Mary;

- a variety of interesting objects/shapes/textures;

- beautiful and/or meaningful pictures, posters, or photos;

- books, poems, or prose that would help reflection and prayer.

❏   Gather aromatic things: perfumes, oils, vaporizers, incense.

❏   Show slides of everyday objects and activities, families, children, aspects of nature, etc.

❏   Display sacramental signs and symbols—water, oil, bread, wheat, wine, grapes, baptismal robe, baptismal candle—at appropriate times.

NOTE: Take care not to overload or clutter the prayer corner or table. Keep it simple but eye-catching!

ALTERNATIVE PLACES FOR PRAYER

❏   Consider using the parish church or school chapel for prayer. Remember it is a special house of God.

❏   Keep in mind the availability of God's natural world of beach, parks, gardens, and even a green area of the school playground. These are all possible sacred places for encountering God in prayer.

LIGHT AND SHADE

Make use of opportunities for bright, filtered, colored, or dimmed lighting as an aid to atmosphere.

BACKGROUND MUSIC

Build up a collection of audio tapes and/or disks—instrumental music, sounds of nature, etc. Soft music quiets children and can be used to signal the beginning of prayer.

FOCUS PHRASES

❏ Display key words and/or phrases from the Bible or from the liturgy in your prayer corner. Some examples might be:

- My God is a fortress and a rock (Ordinary Time).
- Maranatha—Come Lord Jesus (Advent).
- You are Emmanuel, God who is with us (Christmas and new school year).
- Without seeing you, we believe (Ordinary Time).
- If today you hear God's voice, harden not your hearts (Lent).
- Jesus is alive. He is risen. Alleluia (Easter).
- We praise you, we bless you, we thank you God (Ordinary Time).

❏ Display simple prayers or phrases composed by the children as an aid and encouragement to pray, for example:

> Thank you, God, for making me, ME.
> Isn't God great!

❏ Try to create an atmosphere of quiet receptiveness for prayer. Communicating with God requires a certain stillness. It is an art and a skill that comes with practice.

BE STILL AND KNOW THAT I AM GOD.
(Psalm 46:11)

MAKING IT HAPPEN

Prayer is an expression of a child's growing relationship with God, both as an individual and as a member of the faith community. For that relationship to develop fully and harmoniously, the child's experience of prayer needs to be varied and meaningful. The following suggestions will help to make prayer a successful and rewarding classroom experience for you and the children.

- ❏ Make **TIME** for prayer.
- ❏ Choose a time when children are most **RECEPTIVE.**
- ❏ Establish a **PRAYERFUL ATMOSPHERE** and **SIMPLE PRAYER ROUTINES:**
  - Recall the purpose of prayer.
  - Establish prayer signals (Sign of the Cross, lighted candle, quiet music, a moment of silence).
  - Draw attention to the presence of God—in the classroom and in children's hearts.

For where two or three are gathered in my name, I am there among them (Mt 18:20).

❏ KEEP PRAYERS **SHORT**

❏ KEEP THEM **POSITIVE**

❏ KEEP THEM **MEANINGFUL**

❏ Encourage children to talk to God about everyday **JOYS, SORROWS,** and **INTERESTS.**
God made them, knows them, loves them, and is interested in them (Ps 139:1–15).

You are precious in my sight...and I love you.
(Is 43:4)

❏ Use a **VARIETY** of styles and formats for prayer.

SPONTANEOUS prayer

   FORMAL prayer

      PERSONAL and **COMMUNAL** prayer

         IMAGINATIVE prayer (meditation)

            Prayer through **MOVEMENT**

               Prayer in **SONG**

                  VOCAL prayer

                     SILENT prayer

INCLUDE

   Prayers of **PRAISE**

      THANKSGIVING

         SORROW

            BLESSING

               PETITION

❏ **TUNE IN** to where children are:

- God made **ME** (kindergarten).
- God made **EARTH** (grade one/two).
- God made the **GALAXY** (grades four/five).

❏ Relate **LIFE EXPERIENCES** to those of Jesus.

Jesus was fully human. He knows and understands our feelings.

- Jesus celebrated with people and rejoiced with them (wedding at Cana, Jn 2:1–12).
- Jesus cried and was sad (at the death of his friend Lazarus, Jn 11:28–36).
- He was afraid (Mt 26:36–40), angry (Jn 2:13–17), and hurt (Lk 22:54–62).

❏ Read the **SCRIPTURES** regularly.

❏ Help the children to discover that **JESUS PRAYED OFTEN.**

- Alone and in the presence of his disciples (Mk 1:35, Jn 17, Lk 9:18).
- In time of temptation (Lk 4:1–13).
- Before making major decisions (Lk 6:12).
- In thanksgiving (Jn 11:41, Lk 22:16–20).
- Prayers of blessing (Mt 11:25).
- Prayers of petition (Mt 26:39).
- For his friends (Jn 17:11).
- For his enemies (Lk 23:34).

❏ Make a **DAILY TIME** for prayer. It helps to develop a habit of prayer.

❏   Encourage the children to **CREATE THEIR OWN PRAYERS.** Listen carefully to the children's prayers and intentions.

❏   **PRAY OFTEN**. Prayer develops through practice.

❏   **PRAY YOURSELF.** It is most important that the children see you, the teacher, as a person who prays.

❏   **REMEMBER,** you do not need to be a theologian to talk to God or about God.

❏   **HOLD HANDS** often, especially with small children. There is a sense of oneness, security, and comfort in the **TOUCH** of another.

❏   Establish and maintain a **POSITIVE, WARM RELATIONSHIP** with the children.

❏   **BLESS** the children by making a Sign of the Cross on their foreheads, or placing your hands on their heads. Consider the occasional use of holy water or oil as you bless them. This provides a link with the sacramental life of the church.

❏   **PRAY** some simple **BLESSING PRAYERS** over the children, especially at the end of the day. (For examples, see the chapter entitled, "Ending the Day with God.")

❏   Encourage skills of **REFLECTION** and **SILENCE** at other times in the teaching/learning program.

BEGINNING THE DAY WITH GOD

Our faith community has a long tradition of morning prayer. St. Luke (4:42) tells us that when daylight came, Jesus left the house he was staying in and made his way to a lonely place to pray. Throughout the centuries, Christians have gathered in the early morning to offer prayers of praise, thanks, and petition to God. Commencing the day with prayer helps children to focus on God as the source and creator of all life. It reminds them of the loving companionship of God who is always there for them.

While any form of prayer may be used to begin the school day, those of praise, offering, and petition are particularly appropriate for morning prayer. It is useful to begin morning prayer in the classroom with the Sign of the Cross. This provides a traditional starting point for prayer and gives children a way in to conversation with God. Lighting your prayer candle and gathering the class around a prayer table or mat is also an aid in focusing children's attention.

SIGN OF THE CROSS

In the name of the Father and of the Son and of the Holy Spirit. Amen.

A variation of this prayer, which may be useful at times for older children is:

In the name of God my creator, Jesus, my redeemer, and the Holy Spirit, who sanctifies me, I pray...

MORNING OFFERING PRAYERS

Dear Jesus, I offer you today my work, my happiness, and my fears.
Please take care of me, my family, and my friends.

Mary, mother of Jesus and my mother, too,
help me to grow like Jesus in everything I do.

Dear God, we offer you our prayer of praise at the start of another day.
We praise you, we bless you, and we thank you for being our God and our friend.

MORNING SONG

(The verses may be spoken or sung.)

1. Je - sus, Lord, we wish to praise you
2. Bless our friends and school com-pan - ions,
3. Praise you, Lord, for all cre - a - tion,
4. Glo - ry be to God the Fa - ther,

1. And to of - fer you this day
2. Help us all to grow like you.
3. Praise you for your works this day,
4. Glo - ry be to Christ, your Son,

1. All our joys and all our sor - rows,
2. Teach us how to love each oth - er,
3. Praise you for your love and friend - ship,
4. Glo - ry be to the Ho - ly Spi - rit,

1. All our work and all our play.
2. Make us care in all we do.
3. Keep us close to you, we pray.
4. God for ev - er three in one.

BEGINNING PRAYERS

(For little ones)

Je - sus, I love you, be with me to - day.

Bless ev' - ry thing that I do and I say.

PRAYERS OF THE FAITHFUL

Teacher: *Dear Lord, at the start of a new day we come together to praise you, to thank you for your goodness, and to pray to you for all those who are in need....*

Invite children to offer prayers for people in need. It is helpful to use a simple, definite format that both you and the children are comfortable with. It is also helpful for the teacher to begin the prayers with an example for the children to follow. Keep the prayers short and to the point.

For example: *Lord Jesus, please help the people in (name country) to make peace with each other.*
Lord hear us.

Response: *Lord, hear our prayer.*

Lord Jesus, look after my grandmother who is sick today. Lord hear us.

Response: *Lord, hear our prayer.*

Teacher concludes the prayer with such words as:

Father in heaven, we bring you all our prayers today, those we have spoken and those unsaid. We know that you listen and hear our prayers and we entrust them to you through Jesus your Son. Amen.

A LITANY OF PRAISE, THANKS, AND PETITION

Litanies are very easy for the teacher and the children to compose. Like prayers of the faithful, they are participatory in nature and encourage children to join in the composition of the class prayer. Each child may contribute one phrase. Keep the prayer list short and change the response as appropriate.

LEADER	RESPONSE
For the season of ( )	*We praise you, O Lord*
For the sun, moon, and stars	*We praise you, O Lord*
For all of your creatures	*We praise you, O Lord*
For trees and for flowers	*We praise you, O Lord*
For our family and friends	*We thank you, O Lord*
For another new day	*We thank you, O Lord*
For stories and books	*We thank you, O Lord*
For work and for play	*We thank you, O Lord*
For children in hospitals	*We pray to you, Lord*
For those without homes	*We pray to you, Lord*
For the sick and the elderly	*We pray to you, Lord*
For all those alone	*We pray to you, Lord*

For peace in our world	*We ask your help, Lord*
For love in all families	*We ask your help, Lord*
For patience and tolerance	*We ask your help, Lord*
For all of our classmates	*We ask your help, Lord*

Teacher concludes:

All of these prayers, we give you, O Lord.
Take them and hear them, we ask you, O Lord.
For always listening, we thank you, O Lord.
For your love and your mercy, we praise you, O Lord.

You will notice that there is a sense of rhythm and sometimes rhyme in the litany. While neither is necessary, rhythm and/or rhyme can be uplifting, giving the children a feeling of joyfulness and enthusiasm in prayer. A regular meter (beat) also makes it easy for the musically inclined class to sing!

LITANY

(Set to music)

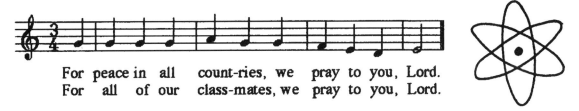

For peace in all count-ries, we pray to you, Lord.
For all of our class-mates, we pray to you, Lord.

LITANIES FOR SPECIAL OCCASIONS

❏   For feasts of Mary:

Invite children to suggest titles or attributes of Mary and compose these into a litany.

Mother of God	*We honor and praise you*
Woman of faith	*We honor and praise you*
Woman of courage	*We honor and praise you*
Mother of Jesus	*We honor and praise you*
Mary most faithful	*Teach us to be like you*
Mary most loving	*Teach us to be like you*
Mary most gentle	*Teach us to be like you*
Mary most kind	*Teach us to be like you*

❑   For the feast of All Saints (November 1st), have children name a favorite saint.

St. Catherine   *Pray for us*

St. Anthony   *Pray for us*

St. Agnes   *Pray for us*

Encourage children to include the names of relatives or friends who have gone before them into God's heavenly kingdom.

❑   For the feast of All Souls (November 2nd), encourage children to name people who have died recently and offer to pray for them in a litany of petition.

For my grandma who died   *We pray to you, Lord*

❑   Invite children to name someone they remember who has died and gone to God's kingdom. When children have finished, pray:

Grant them eternal rest, O Lord, and let the light of your love and peace shine on them now and forever. Amen.

MORNING PRAYER TO THE HOLY SPIRIT

This prayer to the Holy Spirit is especially useful for a confirmation class or around the time of the feast of Pentecost.

Come, O Holy Spirit, come;
Make within our hearts your home;
Guide and strengthen us today;
Help us on our pilgrim way.

Show us how to live anew;
Help us out in all we do;
Be our guide from heaven above;
Teach us goodness, kindness, and love.

Spirit of God be with us today;
Teach us to love, to laugh, and to pray;
Comfort us, strengthen us, help us be good;
So that all things will happen just as they should.

Come, O Holy Spirit, come;
Make within our hearts your home;
Guide and strengthen us today;
Help us on our pilgrim way.

MORNING MEDITATION—GOD IS GOOD

Have children sit in a circle and relax with eyes closed. Invite them to take a moment to think about the people and things around them that make them realize God is good.

AT SCHOOL (playground, friends)

AT HOME (family, toys, good times)

All around them **IN THE WORLD**
(parks, sea, technology, wonderful people, etc.)

Ask the children to choose just one or two things that tell them of God's goodness and to quietly thank God for these things.

Pause for a moment.

When children are ready to open their eyes, invite those who wish to share aloud and name something they would like to thank God for.

Conclude the prayer with a song that expresses the goodness of God.

PRAYING FOR OUR NEEDS

Create a prayer list at the beginning of each week. This helps to overcome the problem of long, never-ending lists of people and things to pray for each day.

A prayer list helps to develop a faith community. It provides an opportunity to tune into the emotional needs of children. It also provides an opportunity to discuss challenges to faith, such as sickness and suffering in our everyday lives, and it reassures children that God is with them at all times.

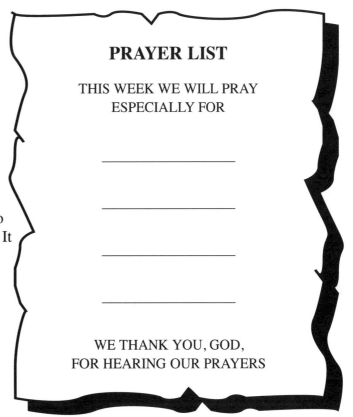

PRAYER LIST

THIS WEEK WE WILL PRAY
ESPECIALLY FOR

_____

_____

_____

_____

WE THANK YOU, GOD,
FOR HEARING OUR PRAYERS

GETTING IN TOUCH: PRAYER STARTERS FOR JOURNAL WRITING

Ask children to close their eyes and imagine that God is very close to them, loving them, and waiting to share a conversation with them.

Tell the children that they can talk to God by completing one or more of the following sentences in their prayer journals.

Dear God,

Today is ...

I feel ...

Today I wish...

I would like to ask you...

I would like to thank you for....

THE OUR FATHER < with movement >

This prayer may be spoken or sung to the familiar plainchant melody used in church or some other well known tune that uses a similar translation.

Our Father,	Bring hands forward palms facing up.
who art in heaven,	Raise hands high.
hallowed be thy name.	Join hands in front of chest.
Thy kingdom come,	Move right hand outward in sweeping motion.
thy will be done, on earth	Move left hand outward in sweeping motion.
as it is in heaven.	Lift both arms high.
Give us this day our daily bread,	Lower hands to receiving position (arms forward, palms facing upwards).
and forgive us our trespasses	Cross arms over chest, lower head.
as we forgive those who trespass against us.	Place arms forward in blessing gesture (palms facing down).
And lead us not into temptation,	Cover eyes with palm of hand.
but deliver us from evil.	Place hands forward, palms upward one on top of the other.
For thine is the kingdom, the power, and the glory	Lift arms up in sweeping motion.
now and forever. Amen.	Join hands in front of chest.

ENDING THE SCHOOL DAY WITH GOD

The end of the day is an excellent time for remembering, for saying thank you, and for making peace with God and one another. A few moments of reflection and prayer can provide a time of healing, of forgiveness, of peace, and of blessing for children. It can send them home feeling good about themselves, about their relationship with God, and about one another.

THINKING IT OVER

At the end of the day after packing up is done, take a few moments to reflect on the day.

- Ask children to quietly recall some of the good things that happened during the day.

- Invite some children to share by naming the thoughts that came to mind.

- Say a prayer of thanksgiving for the good things mentioned and those not mentioned but thought about in the hearts of the children.

- Ask children to think about some of the not so good things that may have happened during the day: nasty words said, untruths told, selfish actions, etc.

- Say a prayer of sorrow, asking God for forgiveness.

OR

- Compose a short litany similar to the "Lord, Have Mercy" used at Mass:

Jesus, you are kind and forgiving.	*Lord, have mercy.*
Jesus, you came to make peace.	*Christ, have mercy.*
Jesus, you want us to be loving toward one another.	*Lord, have mercy.*

Teacher: *May God have mercy on us, forgive us our sins, and bring us to life everlasting.*

All: *Amen.*

OR

- Say an act of sorrow (contrition).

  Traditional:

  O my God, I am very sorry that I have sinned against you because you are so good and with your help I will try not to sin again.

- Share a sign of peace with one another.

- Sing a song of peace.

- Children may compose their own prayers of sorrow and forgiveness.

BLESSING PRAYERS

Blessing prayers are most suitable at the end of the day.

The following are some possibilities:

❏   Say a blessing over the children.

  May God bless you and keep you.
  May God let his face shine upon you and be gracious to you.
  May God bless you and give you peace.

  (Adapted from Num 6:24)

❏   Pray Psalm 67 (66).

❏   Sing blessings with the children to the tune of well-known songs.

  For example: God bless you and God bless me.
  Keep us safe and keep us free.
  God bless Moms and Daddys, too.
  May God bless everything we do.
  God bless you and God bless me.
  Keep us safe and keep us free.

  (Sung to the tune of "Twinkle, Twinkle Little Star.")

❏   As the children leave the classroom, use blessed oil or holy water to make a sign of the cross on their foreheads. Call each child by name and say:
  "God bless you, _____."

❑   Sometimes end the day by making God the *object* of your blessing prayer. You can use some of the verses of the psalms for this.

> *I will bless the Lord at all times.*
> *God's praise shall be ever on my lips (Ps 34:2).*

Other psalms of blessing and praise are Psalms 96, 103, 104, 145.

PRAYER FOR GOD'S PROTECTION

❑   Pray a prayer of reassurance, acknowledging and praising God's protective love:

I lift up my eyes to the mountains:
Who will help me?
My help will come from God,
Who made both the heavens and the earth.

God will never let me stumble or fall
For God never sleeps but is always on guard.
God cares for me and protects me.
Through the day and through the night
God stands beside me.

The Lord is my guardian and protector.
He will keep me from all harm.
The Lord will guard my going and my coming
God takes care of me now and forever.

> *Psalm 121 (adapted for children)*

NOTE
When using the psalms with children, it is important to choose suitable verses. At times it may be appropriate to exercise a degree of freedom with regard to the translation. Each of the psalms suggested in this chapter is available in the *Lectionary For Masses With Children*, published by the authority of the commission on Liturgy, National Conference of Catholic Bishops.

The psalms are a marvelous source for prayer. A little courage and some personal research will make this manifest.

❑   Encourage children to write their own psalms of praise, thanks, and blessing **OR** their own translations of the psalms. Pray these at the end of the day.

ECHO PRAYERS

Echo prayers or "say after me" prayers are useful when praying with very young children or at the end of a tiring day. Try these:

Thank you, God, for another day (children repeat).
Bless you, God, for your love and care (children repeat).
Praise you, God, for this beautiful world (children repeat).
Keep us and protect us from all harm (children repeat).

(Begin and end the prayer segment with the Sign of the Cross.)

Teacher and/or children can lead these prayers. It is important to limit the number to just a few.

USING AN AROMA TO END THE DAY OR FOR A SPECIAL OCCASION

❑   EUCALYPTUS

- Put a few drops of eucalyptus in a heat proof bowl and place on a decorated prayer table or mat. (If possible decorate the table with leaves and/or flowering branches).

- Take a moment to reflect on the events of the day.

- Have the children silently think of something good to offer to God.

- Have the children think of something that needs forgiveness or healing.

   (The children could name some things that are significant for them if they wish.)

- Pour some hot water into the bowl. A delightful aroma of eucalyptus vapor should rise from the bowl and begin to fill the room.

- Pray a prayer on behalf of the class, for example:

Dear God,

As the eucalyptus vapor rises into the air, we give to you all the moments of our day with all its ups and downs: the happiness, the frustrations, the laughter, the fun, the friendships, the tears (if appropriate). We offer you the beautiful fragrance of the good things that have happened in our class today and we ask you to heal the hurts and forgive any selfishness in our actions.

We thank you for the eucalypti trees, which help us make this prayer to you. Help us to treasure each day of our lives, all of our world, and each other.

We make our prayer in Jesus' name. Amen.

❏   INCENSE

Burn some incense or an incense stick and make a similar prayer of fragrant offering to God.

OR

Pray some verses from Psalm 141.

> *At the end of the day, we call upon you, Lord.*
> *Come and listen to us.*
> *Let our prayer rise before you like incense in your sight,*
> *And may the lifting up of our hands be an evening offering to you.*
> *Amen.*
>
> *(Free translation)*

IMAGINATIVE PRAYER

In the gospel of Luke, at the end of the story of the young boy Jesus lost and then found teaching in the temple, we read these words:

His mother (Mary) treasured all these things in her heart (Lk 2:51).

To treasure, to ponder, to think, to meditate, and to use our imaginations to converse with God are time-honored traditions in our Christian faith. Guided meditation as a form of prayer enables us to share this tradition with our children. Imaginative prayer or meditation is suitable for children of all ages.

❏   Through guided reflection on everyday objects and events, the teacher can assist children in recognizing and encountering God in their everyday lives in a personal and intimate manner.

❏   Christian meditation or imaginative prayer can:

- Provide an opportunity for children to hear and respond to the Word of God in the scriptures.

- Give children time and space to enter into conversation and friendship with God through the person of Jesus.

- Assist the children in discovering the presence of God within them, thus enabling them to meet God deep within their hearts.

GUIDED MEDITATION

Christian meditation or imaginative prayer acknowledges the gift and the power of the Holy Spirit at work in each of us to bring about a deeper knowledge of God and a greater closeness to the author of all life and being.

There are four basic steps in the process:

RELAX

FOCUS

PONDER

PRAY

STEP ONE: RELAX

Successful imaginative prayer requires that the children be relaxed but alert. This can be achieved by establishing a relaxation routine which is reasonably quick and easy to accomplish. The following listening and breathing exercises are common ways of helping children to enter into a relaxed but alert state of mind. Note: the children may be sitting or lying down.

❏ LISTENING EXERCISE

Instruct the children:

- Make yourself comfortable so that nothing is bothering you.
- Close your eyes and let your body feel peaceful and relaxed.
- Take a few deep breaths and let all of the tightness and tension drain out of you. Like a floppy rag doll, let your body become loose and relaxed.
- Now become aware of your ears.
- Listen to the sounds around you.
- What sounds can you hear close by you in the room?
- Picture these sounds and name them to yourself.

Pause for a few seconds.

- Now let your ears pick up all the sounds you can hear outside the room.
- Listen carefully to these sounds and once again name them to yourself.

Pause for a few seconds.

- Now turn your attention far away into the distance.
- How many sounds can you hear? (To assist children, teacher may name an audible place such as a highway that may be close by or a shopping center).

Pause again for a few seconds.

❏ BREATHING EXERCISE

Teacher continues the instruction:

- Now focus on your breathing.
- Feel the air coming into your body through your nose, traveling deep down into your lungs, and then coming out again through your mouth.
- Concentrate on your breathing for a few minutes, enjoying the way the air passes into your body and out again, filling you with energy and life.
- Breathe in and out a few times slowly and peacefully and feel happy with yourself.

STEP TWO: FOCUS

In this phase the children focus all their attention on a concrete object before them and explore its attributes. (The object may be something they have created or have collected: a stone, a leaf, a drawing, a toy from home, or something that they use at school. There are no limits as everything is a source of prayer and conversation with God to those who believe in God's nearness and presence.)

Direct the children with such statements and questions as:

- Hold your object in your hand and look closely at it.

- What does it feel like? Is it rough, smooth, etc.?

- What can you see? What colors are present?

- Where do you think it came from?

- Do you have other objects like this at home?

- What do you like about your object?

STEP THREE: PONDER

In this part of the guided meditation direct children to thoughts associated with the object. Instruct them to place the object on the floor or desk in front of them and to close their eyes.

Ask questions such as:

- When you think about your object, what does it remind you of?

- Does your object remind you of someone you love?

- Does your object tell you something about God?

- Does your object tell you something about yourself?

STEP FOUR: PRAY

This is the main part of the meditation. In this phase, encourage the children to:

- Enter their heart or a special place in their imagination where they can talk with Jesus using the object as a theme for the prayer.

- Share with Jesus their personal thoughts and feelings about the object of the meditation or anything else they may wish to share with him.

- Listen silently to what Jesus might say to them in reply.

  (Pause for a few seconds.)

To close the meditation, it is important to gently bring the children back to the classroom situation by using the breathing exercises outlined above.

GETTING STARTED: SOME SUGGESTIONS FOR IMAGINATIVE PRAYER

GOD IN NATURE

❏   Ask the children to provide an object from nature or supply one yourself (e.g., a leaf, twig, flower, stone, pine cone, shell, sand, etc.).

❏   With some quiet music in the background, take the children through the relaxation routine. (Relax)

❏   Ask the children to take their object in their hands.

- Is it hard/soft, smooth/rough, bright/dull, complicated/simple, large/small?

- Does it have a smell?

- What does it tell you about God?

- Is God like this object in any way?

- What does it tell you about yourself?

- Are you like this object in any way?

- Turn to God in your heart.

- What would you like to say to God right now?

- Does God say anything back to you?

(pause)

- When you have finished talking with God, you may want to say goodbye for now. When you are ready, open your eyes and return to the classroom.

❏   The children may wish to share some of their responses. Sometimes discussion is helpful.

❏   Conclude with a short echo prayer. (Children repeat each line.)
We thank you, God, for the beauty of your creation.
Together we offer you glory and praise.
We thank you, God, for making us.

❏   The class may pray together:
Glory be to the Father and to the Son and to the Holy Spirit, as it was in the beginning, is now, and ever shall be, forever and ever. Amen.

GRATITUDE FOR FOOD

❏   Ask the children to sit in a circle with a drawing or a picture of a favorite food.

❏   Have them name the food they have chosen and share what they like about it.

❑ Have the children turn the picture down on the floor in front of them, close their eyes, and relax.

❑ Ask the children to think of the most recent time they had this favorite food to eat.

- Can you remember where you were?
- Who was with you?
- What were you doing?
- Was it a special occasion?
- Were you with your family or with friends?

❑ Continue:

- Imagine you are sharing this time again now.
- Jesus is with you, too. He likes to share in your happy times of eating and having fun with friends.
- Talk to him about your favorite food and your family and friends.
- Thank him for food and for your friends and ask him to bless you all.
- Watch him as he raises his hand to bless you and the food you are sharing.

❑ Bring children gently back to the classroom situation and ask them to turn their picture over and look at it again.

❑ Children may want to put their pictures on the wall or the refrigerator at home to remind them that God gives them good food and family and friends to share it.

MY FAVORITE TOY

❑ Encourage the children to bring to class or think about a favorite toy.

❑ Have the children relax and close their eyes.

❑ Lead the class into the meditation:

- Think about your special toy. What is it?
- When did you get it?
- Why is it special to you?
- Who gave it to you?
- Does your favorite toy remind you of a special person? When do you play with it?
- Where do you keep your toy? Does it have a special place? Does it have a name?
- Take a moment to talk to Jesus about your toy. Jesus is interested in the things that are important to you.

- Tell Jesus why your toy is special to you.

  (Pause)

- What does Jesus think of your toy?

- Listen as he tells you that it took many people to make your special toy. Hear him say he is happy that you like it and that you treasure it as something special.

  (Pause)

- Ask Jesus to bless those who made your toy and those who gave it to you.

  (Pause)

- When you go home today, take your toy and look at it. Remember that you thought about it today and you prayed for those who made it and gave it to you. Look after it because it is a special sign of someone's love for you.

❑ Lead children gently back to the classroom situation.

❑ Children may wish to share some of their thoughts with each other or with the class.

PHOTO PRAYERS

❑ Sit the children in a circle around a prayer mat upon which you have displayed a series of photos or pictures of various objects, people, and events.

❑ Invite children to choose one of the photos/pictures for reflection and prayer. You may suggest a particular theme (e.g., friendship, forgiveness, God, happiness, sadness, peace, etc.).

❑ Allow the children to share something about the particular photo/picture they have chosen.

❑ Ask the children to close their eyes and to spend a few moments talking with Jesus about the picture they have chosen.

❑ Pass a lighted candle around the group and invite the children to share a prayer with the class.

❑ Conclude the prayer session with a general prayer that includes some of the reflections of the children.

SHARING A LIFE MOMENT WITH JESUS

❑ Begin with a relaxation and breathing exercise.

❑ Invite the children to close their eyes and recall a happy time that they have recently experienced.

❏   Help children to relive the moment by focusing their attention on some of the details.

- Recall the place of your happy experience (home, playground, party, beach, etc.).
- Are you alone or with family or friends?
- Recall the things around you—the physical surroundings (furniture, trees, flowers, sand, comfortable chair, party room, backyard, favorite place, etc.).
- Listen to the sounds around you (talking, wind, sea, rustling of leaves, people laughing, etc.)

❏   Suggest to children that they can invite Jesus to join them for a few moments and share their happiness.

❏   Continue:

- Say something to Jesus to welcome him.
- How do you feel?
- What does Jesus say? Perhaps he is just happy to be with you!
- Are you happy to include him?
- Do you want to say anything further to him? Perhaps you would like to share with him what you are doing. (Pause between each of the suggestions to allow time for a response.)

❏   After a few moments, suggest that children allow Jesus to leave them. They may imagine him going off into the distance. They might like to say "goodbye" or just let him disappear from their sight.

❏   Gently bring the children back into the classroom situation by instructing them to concentrate once again on their breathing. When they are ready, invite them to open their eyes.

❏   Invite those who wish to share something of their experience.

MEDITATING ON THE GOSPEL STORIES

❏   Lead the children through a relaxation exercise.

❏   Create a gospel scene for the children. Invite them to become one of the characters in the story.

Some questions for reflection and prayer might be:

- Who are you in the story?
- Where are you? Are you close to Jesus?
- Who else is in the story?

- Can Jesus see you?
- Is he speaking to you?
- What is he saying to you?
- How do you respond?
- Listen to Jesus. He may have a special message for you. (Pause) Take a moment to praise and thank Jesus for his message to you.

❏ Children may want to record their special message in a prayer journal or diary.

VARIATION ON A GOSPEL MEDITATION

❏ Ask the children to sit quietly, to relax, and to close their eyes.

❏ Lead the children into the prayer.

- Imagine that you are surrounded only by darkness.
- Listen to the sounds around you. (pause)
- Picture the classroom in your mind. (pause)
- Picture in your mind your best friend or the teacher.
- Imagine what it would be like if you were blind and unable to see these things or people again!
- Now listen to the story I am going to read.
- Imagine that you are there in the story, watching Jesus.

❏ Read Mark 10:46–52, "The Healing of Bartimaeus." (Read slowly and pause between each verse).

❏ At the end of the story, invite children to say something quietly to Jesus about what he just did for the blind man. (Allow a few moments of silence for this.)

❏ Invite children to open their eyes and to thank God for the gift of sight.

The gospel stories easily lend themselves to imaginative prayer. Numerous scenes might be selected by the teacher and used as a basis for guided meditation.

The four steps

RELAX ⟶ **FOCUS** ⟶ **PONDER** ⟶ **and** ⟶ **PRAY**

enable the teacher to lead the children into private conversation with Jesus and to invite God into their everyday lives in a personal and intimate manner.

THE ROSARY—SHORT MEDITATIONS ON THE LIFE OF JESUS

The Rosary is another form of meditation the children can pray. It is best prayed in small segments—perhaps one decade at a time.

❑   Choose one of the mysteries of the Rosary and read or tell the children the story from the gospels.

❑   Invite the children to ponder on the story as you lead them in saying one Our Father, ten Hail Mary's, and the Glory Be.

The Mysteries of the Rosary are divided into three groups each with five segments:

JOYFUL

The Annunciation

The Visitation

The Birth of Jesus

The Presentation of Jesus in the Temple

The Finding of Jesus in the Temple

SORROWFUL

The Agony in the Garden

The Scourging at the Pillar

The Crowning with Thorns

The Carrying of the Cross

The Crucifixion

GLORIOUS

The Resurrection

The Ascension

The Coming of the Holy Spirit

The Assumption of Mary into Heaven

The Crowning of Mary, Queen of Heaven

PRAYING ALWAYS: MANTRAS AND OTHER IDEAS

Jesus prayed often. He told his disciples a parable about their need to pray always and not to lose heart (Lk 18:1–8). The early Christians knew the importance of prayer in the development of a lifelong relationship with God and each other. Paul, writing to the people of Thessalonica, exhorts them to rejoice always and to pray without ceasing (1 Thess 5:17).

There are many ways of developing an attitude of prayerfulness and an abiding sense of the presence of God in our lives. In this chapter you will find a collection of prayer ideas that have been found helpful in deepening one's relationship with and awareness of God.

MANTRAS

A mantra is a holy name, word, or phrase which you repeat often, letting it run through your mind as you breathe, work, and play.

❑ Choose a short phrase that is easy to say or sing and teach it to the children. Call on this phrase at various times during the day. It will provide a precious moment of prayer amid all the hustle and bustle of classroom activity.

SUGGESTIONS FOR THE DIFFERENT SEASONS OF THE CHURCH YEAR

These phrases may be spoken or sung.

Advent

Ma-ra-na-tha, ma - ra-na- tha, come Lord Je- sus, come.

Advent ⟨ simpler version ⟩

Come, Lord Je - sus, come to us.

Christmas

Je - sus, born on Christ - mas day,

Teach us how to love and pray.

Lent

If to - day you hear God's voice

Har - den not your hearts ------------- .

Encourage the children to choose their own mantra (a name for God, a phrase that they really like from the Bible, a psalm verse, or a phrase from a favorite hymn) and to repeat this name or phrase as often as they think of it.

TRY THIS EXPERIMENT

Invite children:

- Choose a place where you can sit quietly and let your special word or phrase run calmly through your mind. This place could be inside or outside the classroom.
- Keep repeating your special phrase over and over in your mind while you try some small action (e.g., straightening your socks or untying and tying your shoelace).
- Get up and take a short walk. Keep repeating your phrase slowly in your mind.
- Find something to do (e.g., tidy your desk, pick a flower, scribble on a pad, play with a ball). See if you can keep your phrase or word running through your mind.

Discuss the experiment:

- How did it go?
- It gets better with practice.
- Remember, God is always with us.

PRESENCE OF JESUS PRAYER

Choose a moment when the children are reasonably inactive, perhaps at the end of a lesson or the beginning of a new one.

- When the children are settled, remind them that we believe Jesus is always present with us through his spirit living in us. Jesus is with us right now.
- Suggest that the children try to be still for a few moments and tune in to the presence of Jesus.
- Invite them to imagine that they are like a large sponge that soaks in water, but they will soak in all the love that Jesus has for them.
- Have children take a big breath and soak up all of the love that Jesus has for each one of them. (Pause for a few seconds.)

With some small variations, this presence of Jesus prayer can be used often (perhaps using the image of an empty vessel, water well, etc.).

PRESENCE OF GOD SONGS

Provide time for the children to listen to songs that remind them of the presence and closeness of God.

SHARING SILENCE WITH JESUS

❑   Ask children to close their eyes and put their heads down on their desks and imagine for a few moments that they are alone with Jesus who loves them. Allow them some time to talk to Jesus in their hearts.

❑   Take the children out to the playground or to a quiet area of the school. Invite them to be still and to listen to the silence. Talk with the children about what silence feels like and sounds like.

It is important that children learn to handle silence.

PRAYER BEFORE LUNCH

Make the Sign of the Cross.

Thank you, God, for the food we are about to eat.

Thank you for friends to share it with.

Bless us and bless those who prepared our lunch.

Help us to be good friends with each other.

In the name of the Father...

ACTS OF FAITH IN THE PRESENCE OF JESUS WITHIN ME

Share these short prayers with the children.

• *Jesus, I believe that I have your Spirit living within me. Help me to remember this and to draw on the strength and wisdom of the Holy Spirit in all the things I do.*

• *Holy Spirit of Jesus living within my heart, fill me with your light, your strength, and your love.*

• *Jesus, I believe that you are with me and that you hear my prayers. Today I want to pray for...*

NOTES OR LETTERS TO GOD

Explain to the children that God is interested in everything that is important to them. As they are learning and developing writing skills, encourage them to practice their skills by writing notes or letters to God. Older children can do a similar exercise in a diary or prayer journal.

- Invite children to tell God something that is important to them right now (e.g., "Dear God, I learned how to ride a bike this week," or, "I lost another tooth," or, "My puppy is sick, please help him.").

- Make a mailbox for depositing letters or notes to God. Establish a means of sending the notes to God, for example, by carrying them in procession to the prayer table.

- At a suitable time, burn the notes or offer them to God at a class eucharist.

DOODLE PRAYER

This prayer form allows children to use paper and crayons, markers, or pencils to doodle or scribble and then see if their drawing has meaning for them. This meaning may be shared with God in prayer.

- Provide each child with some drawing tools and a large piece of paper.

- Play some quiet, reflective music and tell children that they have as much time as they need (about 10-15 minutes) to doodle or draw something on their piece of paper.

- When the time is sufficient, invite children to share their drawing with a partner. The sharing and the explanation to each other help to draw meaning from the scribble or the drawing.

- Encourage children to turn the page over and write a prayer on the reverse side, sharing something of their discovery or feelings with God. Alternatively, allow children to close their eyes and share their prayer or thoughts with God.

- Some children may wish to share their prayers with the class. Do not force this, but allow some sharing for those who express a desire to do so.

PRAYING WITH SCRIPTURE

Select an appropriate passage from the Bible. Be sure not to make it too long.

- Read the passage once and invite children to listen quietly.

- Read the passage a second time. This time invite children to listen for a word or a phrase that strikes them or stands out for them.

- Invite children in turn to share their word or phrase aloud.

- Read the passage a third time and invite children to offer a short, one-sentence prayer incorporating their word or phrase or something associated with either.

- Have children respond to each prayer with the word *Amen*.

PRAYER IN ACTION: A DAILY FOCUS FOR PRAYER

Genuine prayer leads to a fuller and more faithful Christian life. A prayerful relationship with God constantly challenges us to live more like Jesus did by trying to fulfill more perfectly the great commandments of love of God and love of neighbor, not only in our prayers but also in our actions.

> *Let that same mind be in you that was in Christ Jesus (Phil 2:5).*

> *Faith without works is dead (Jas 2:14).*

The Daily Christian Living program suggested in this chapter is one practical way of focusing attention on the link between prayer and action, between what we say and what we do.

DAILY CHRISTIAN LIVING

Beginning with Sunday, each day is allocated particular aspects or characteristics of Christian living. These aspects of Christian life become the focus for prayer and for action during the day.

NOTE: You may find that a five-day week rather than seven is more suitable for younger children. A modified program for young children is also provided.

THE PROGRAM

SUNDAY	MONDAY	TUESDAY	WEDNESDAY	THURSDAY	FRIDAY	SATURDAY
Celebrating and Recreating	Showing Love	Giving Thanks and Caring for Earth	Being Just	Living with Suffering	Forgiving and Making Up	Making Peace

SUNDAY

Celebrating
and
Recreating

In the Christian tradition, Sunday is the day when we celebrate our faith and take time to renew and recreate our energies through relaxation and recreation activities.

(On) six days shall work be done, but the seventh is a Sabbath of complete rest, a holy convocation...a Sabbath to the Lord (Lev 23:3).

PRAYER: *Dear Jesus,*

> *We praise and thank you for the gift of faith, for the Sabbath holiday, and for the people in our church family who help us to grow in our relationship with you.*
>
> *Today we thank you especially for the gift of yourself in the Eucharist.*
>
> *Help us to celebrate Sunday with prayer and with joy.*

ACTION: We make a special effort to pray with all God's people by celebrating the Eucharist together.

We take time to relax and to have fun with family and friends.

MONDAY

Showing
Love

Jesus said:

This is my commandment, that you love one another as I have loved you (Jn 15:12).

More than anything else, Jesus wants us to be loving people.

PRAYER: Say or sing the first two verses of the Morning Song (p.13).

> *Dear Jesus,*
>
> *Help us today to be kind and loving toward everyone at school.*
>
> *Teach us how to be thoughtful of others and to be unselfish in the decisions we make and the actions we take.*
>
> *We pray especially for people who are unloved...*

(Pause and allow time for shared or silent prayer. You might want to suggest or invite particular prayers).

ACTION: We make a special effort to be caring, kind, and generous toward others.

TUESDAY

Giving Thanks and Caring for Earth

Everything we have is God's gift to us. St Paul tells us:

Give thanks to God the Father at all times and for everything in the name of Our Lord Jesus Christ (Eph 5:20).

Gratitude is an important Christian virtue—one that fosters humility and encourages a right relationship with God. Gratitude helps us to treasure and care for the many gifts we receive from God.

PRAYER: Sing or say some verses of the Morning Song (p. 13).

> *Dear God,*
>
> *We thank you for your beautiful creation, for the sea, the flowers, the birds, and the trees.*
>
> *We thank you for giving each one of us life.*
>
> *We thank you for our families, our teachers, and our friends.*
>
> *Most of all, we thank you for being our God and our friend. Help us today to remember that everything is a gift. Help us to show respect for our world and to say thank you.*

ACTION: We make a special effort to be grateful people by caring for our world and by saying thank you to God, to our parents, our teachers, and our friends for all that they do for us.

WEDNESDAY

Being Just

Through the words of the prophet Micah, God asks us to:

> *live justly,*
> *love tenderly, and*
> *walk humbly with God (Mic 6:8).*

When we act justly, we help to bring about God's reign upon the earth. We help to establish God's kingdom of justice, love, and peace for everyone.

PRAYER: *Dear Jesus,*

Teach us the true meaning of justice and its importance for the well-being and happiness of all peoples. Help us to be tolerant and fair to everyone we meet.

We pray especially for people who are treated unjustly...

ACTION: We make a special effort to be tolerant, fair, and just at home, in the classroom, and on the playground.

THURSDAY

Living with Suffering

Jesus said:

If any want to become my followers, let them deny themselves and take up their cross daily and follow me (Lk 9:23).

Disappointments, hurts, pain, and suffering are a part of life. Jesus knew and experienced this. Through his death and resurrection he teaches us that there is a positive, redemptive side to suffering—that we can grow and become strong through the sad and difficult times in our lives. Jesus gives us his Spirit to help us grow through the hard things we experience.

PRAYER: Say or sing the first verse of the Morning Song (p.13).

Dear Jesus,

Help us today to be strong in following you. Help us to put up with the hurts and difficulties that come our way without complaining because, Jesus, you did this for each one of us.

We pray for the sick and those who are hurting in their hearts.

ACTION: We make a special effort to accept without complaining the little things that annoy and hurt us. We use the hard things of the day to make us strong in body, mind, and spirit.

We unite our sufferings with those of Jesus, who died to save us from our sins.

FRIDAY

Forgiving and
Making up

Being forgiven and offering forgiveness to others is an important Christian action.

Jesus said:

If you forgive others...your heavenly Father will also forgive you (Mt 6:14), and from the cross he prayed:

Father forgive them for they do not know what they are doing (Lk 23:34).

PRAYER: Sing or say some verses of the "Morning Song" (p.13).

> *Dear Jesus,*
>
> *Help us today to forgive all those who have hurt us.*
>
> *Forgive me for my own sins and acts of selfishness and help me to make friends with those that I have hurt in any way.*

ACTION: We make a special effort to forgive and make up with anyone who hurts us today.

SATURDAY

Making
Peace

Peace is Jesus' gift to us.

Peace I leave with you, my peace I give to you (Jn 14:27).

Kingdom people are people who work for peace. God's kingdom of peace comes from right living. God wants us to help bring about peace in our world by praying for peace, by being peacemakers, and by doing what we know is right.

Saturday is the day when many Christians honor Mary, mother of Jesus and our mother. One of her titles is Queen of Peace. Saturday is a good day to remember Mary and to pray with her for peace in our hearts, our homes, and our world.

PRAYER: Say the Hail Mary followed by the aspiration,

> *Mary, Queen of Peace, pray for us.*

ACTION: We make a special effort to be peacemakers at home.

MODIFIED PROGRAM ‹ For younger children ›

MONDAY	TUESDAY	WEDNESDAY	THURSDAY	FRIDAY
Love	Thank	Pray	Be Fair	Make Peace

❑ Begin each day with the Sign of the Cross, followed by the Christian Living Song (next page).

> **NOTE:** The words of the song can be spoken or sung. Children clap hands on the words underlined.

❑ Conclude each prayer time with the Sign of the Cross.

MONDAY

Love

PRAYER: *Dear Jesus, teach us how to love—to be friends with each other and friends with God.*

ACTION: Today we will show our love by playing happily together, sharing our toys and games with each other, giving our moms and dads a hug.

TUESDAY

Thank

PRAYER: *Dear Jesus, we thank you for our beautiful world, for all the gifts we are given, and for all the good things that people do for us.*

ACTION: Today we will try to remember to say thank you to everyone who helps us.

Christian Living Song

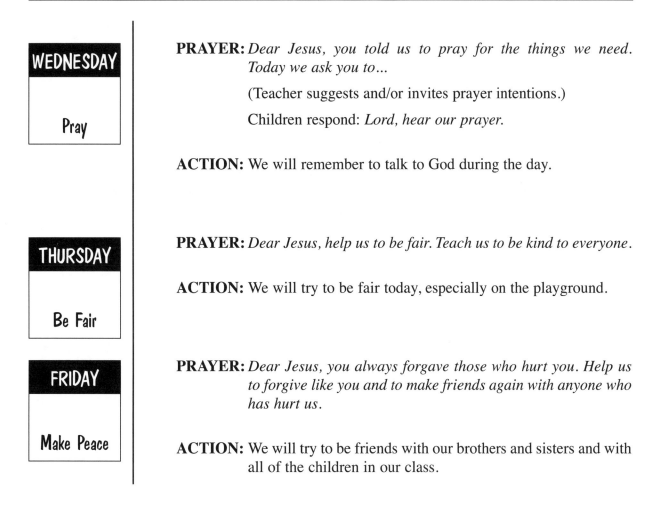

WEDNESDAY

Pray

PRAYER: *Dear Jesus, you told us to pray for the things we need. Today we ask you to...*

(Teacher suggests and/or invites prayer intentions.)

Children respond: *Lord, hear our prayer.*

ACTION: We will remember to talk to God during the day.

THURSDAY

Be Fair

PRAYER: *Dear Jesus, help us to be fair. Teach us to be kind to everyone.*

ACTION: We will try to be fair today, especially on the playground.

FRIDAY

Make Peace

PRAYER: *Dear Jesus, you always forgave those who hurt you. Help us to forgive like you and to make friends again with anyone who has hurt us.*

ACTION: We will try to be friends with our brothers and sisters and with all of the children in our class.

You might want to put up a flash card or similar sign each day in a prominent place (perhaps the prayer table or corner). The card serves as a reminder to the children of the practice for the day. Children may be given the responsibility of changing the card each day.

CREATIVE MOVEMENT

C reative movement allows children to express praise, love, joy, thanks, sorrow, faith, and petition through movement and dance. It enables them to become aware of how they can express thoughts, moods, and emotions as prayer using their bodies as well as their minds. When music is used, the children are encouraged to listen to it with their whole being, not just hearing it, but moving or dancing to it, allowing it to transform them by its rhythm and mood.

Creative movement helps the children to understand that they can communicate with God in many different ways involving all aspects of their person.

Sing to the Lord a new song,

Sing God's praise in the assembly of the faithful.

Let the children of God rejoice in their King.

Let them praise God with music and dancing,

Make melody to God with tambourine and harp (Psalm 149:1–3).

USING A SCRIPTURE PASSAGE

Choose a scripture passage involving imagery, such as:

- the Creation Story (Gen 1:1–5)
- the Storm on the Lake (Mk 4:35–41)
- the Parable of the Sower (Mk 4:1–10)
- the Valley of Dry Bones (Ezek 37:1–10)

Read the story and allow time for reflection.

Read the story again and encourage the children to express the story in movement. Where helpful, play some suitable mood music as background. Props such as material, scarves, foliage, candles, etc., may be used to enhance the movement.

At the end of the story, encourage stillness and a personal, prayerful response to the action. The response may be silent or shared.

MOOD MUSIC

❑ Choose a piece of classical, instrumental music which suggests a particular mood such as joy, excitement, sadness, growth, etc.

Have the children listen to the music and try to *feel* the mood.

Play the music a second time and encourage the children to express the mood of the music through movement. They may like to offer their movement/dance to God as prayer.

MOVEMENT AND SONG

❑ Encourage the children to explore the words of sacred songs/hymns that they like to sing.

Invite them in groups to create gestures or movements to express the sentiments of the lyrics.

Allow time for each group to present its song/hymn as a prayer involving both movement and song.

OR

❑ Have the students listen to a song or hymn that lends itself to movement or action.

Allow the students to spontaneously create movements to the words and music as a form of prayer.

FOLK DANCE

❑ Consider folk dancing for God as a form of prayer.

Use songs that have simple rhythms and easily remembered words.

Folk Dance Steps

Have students find a partner and form a single circle.

To the words of the song:

- Students join hands in the circle and take seven steps to the right, stamping their feet twice on the eighth beat.
- Repeat step one to the left.
- Students clap hands with their partner twice, then slap own knees twice and clap own hands once.
- Students clap hands with their partner again, twice, then link arms and dance around in a small circle to end the sequence.
- Repeat as desired.

For a variation, change partners for each sequence by turning a half circle only for step 4.

NOTE: Those teachers who are good dancers might like to consider creating some basic dance steps to some of the children's religious songs.

Praise songs with a four-beat rhythm or meter can be enjoyable and prayerful when accompanied by dance-type movements.

PRAYER POSTURES

Prayer in all its forms can be prayed using any posture. However, particular postures do tend to lend themselves to specific prayer attitudes and may assist in the expression of those attitudes to God.

❏   Discuss different postures for prayer and encourage children to experiment with them. Try some of these in class:

PRAYER POSTURE	SUGGESTED PRAYER ATTITUDES/ACTION
Standing	active, dignified, respectful
Kneeling	expressing adoration, sorrow, and penance
Sitting	listening, relaxing, and enjoying the presence of God
Lying on stomach or back	meditation or imaginative prayer
Sitting cross-legged	alert but comfortable for communicating with God
Walking	thoughtful, repetitive prayer (mantras)

| Sitting with hands in lap, palms upward | expressing acceptance or petition and need |
| Holding hands with others | expressing oneness and unity with God and one another |

Discuss with the children how they feel when they assume different postures for prayer.

Allow the children to choose the posture that appeals to them most and to spend a few moments in silent prayer.

THE TABLEAU

Creating a tableau in groups, by oneself, or with a partner can assist prayer.

❏ Tell or read a scripture story, pausing at each new step or action in the story. As you read, encourage the children to become one of the characters in the story and to form a still sculpture or tableau for each stage of the journey through the story.

At the end of the story, allow a few moments of silence for children to share with God their own feelings.

❏ During Holy Week, designate different groups of children to form tableaux for the Stations of the Cross. Pray the Stations using each tableau as a focus for prayer.

LIVING SCULPTURES

❏ Invite the children to choose a partner with whom they can work sensibly and comfortably.

Discuss with the children some of the attributes that Jesus recommends for all Christians:

gratitude	forgiveness
humility	prayerfulness
compassion	love
strength	faith
kindness	blessing
gentleness	petition
praise	sorrow

Recall some examples from the gospels or from experience that illustrate these characteristics.

Invite one child from each pair to assume the role of sculptor and the other to be the clay with whom the sculptor will work.

Play some quiet music and encourage children to create a piece of sculpture to represent one of the attributes discussed as a prayer offering to God.

After a few moments allow the children to identify their work and to admire that of other classmates.

If appropriate, children may then exchange roles and repeat the prayer exercise.

PROCESSIONS

Processions assist prayer by focusing attention on the activity at hand and by encouraging a prayerful attitude in the participants as they move from place to place. Processions may also form part of the prayer activity itself.

Try these suggestions:

❏   GUARD OF HONOR

Have the children welcome the Word of God into their midst by forming a guard of honor. The children begin by standing in two rows, facing each other, with their hands by their sides or behind their backs.

As the book bearer and candle bearers process through the two rows, the children bring their hands to the front and hold them out in a receiving position, palms upward.

When the Bible has arrived at the prayer table, children drop hands to sides and move in procession to form a semicircle around the table. They sit and place hands on laps, with palms facing upward in a receiving position to listen to the Word of God.

This action is enhanced by the singing of a favorite hymn.

❏   PALM SUNDAY

On the Monday of Holy Week, invite children to bring green foliage, handmade palms, green streamers, posters, or placards to wave in a procession of praise and triumph for Jesus.

The procession may be headed by a child carrying an image of Jesus: a picture, a statue, or a crucifix that has been decorated in regal colors to emphasize the kingship of Christ.

Have the children walk in procession around a designated space in the school grounds or in the church singing praise songs, hymns, or chanting suitable phrases, such as, "Jesus is our King. We will follow him."

PRAYER SERVICES

Paraliturgies or prayer services are an excellent means of linking personal and communal prayer to the liturgical prayer of the church community. Loosely based on the Liturgy of the Word at Mass, these prayer forms are most suitable as a conclusion to a topic studied in class or to celebrate a national day, a feast day of the church year, or a special day such as World Environment Day, Mother's Day, or Universal Children's Day.

Paraliturgies are most successful when teacher and children plan and prepare them together. A suggested format for a prayer service or paraliturgy is:

GATHER ——————▶ FOCUS ——————▶ REFLECT ——————▶ RESPOND

❑ GATHER

Begin with a gathering ritual:

- a song
- a relaxation exercise
- the taking up of a prayer position
- the lighting of a candle

❑ FOCUS

Focus the children's attention on the theme or object of the prayer:

- a feast day
- a symbol
- a particular topic
- a life experience
- a season of the church year

Read, tell, or have the children dramatize an appropriate scripture story or passage.

NOTE: It is important always to connect the theme of the prayer with the Christian story as found in the scriptures and in the life and teachings of Jesus.

❑ REFLECT

Reflect on the meaning of the theme or the Word for the children's lives today. This may be done by:

• pondering the ideas in silence (teacher provides one or two questions to guide the thinking)

• sharing ideas

• writing thoughts and/or prayers suggested by the theme and/or readings

❑ RESPOND

Encourage children to make a response in word and/or action to the theme through:

• prayers of praise, thanks, wonder, love, sorrow, petition, adoration

• actions of kindness, care for Earth, justice, fairness, gentleness, patience

Conclude the prayer session with a song related to the theme.

JESUS, THE LIGHT OF THE WORLD

(A prayer service for schools and parish religious education groups to celebrate Candlemas Day, February 2nd.)

❑ GATHER

• Arrange a table with a decorated cloth and sufficient candles for distribution—one for each class.

• Place on the table a Bible, a bowl of holy water, and a sprig of foliage for sprinkling the water.

• Gather the children into the assembly area.

• Use reflective music to create an atmosphere of quiet and readiness for prayer.

❑ FOCUS

• Explain to the children the Christian tradition of blessing candles on Candlemas Day. Tell them that they have come together for the blessing of their class candles, which will be used at prayer times throughout the year.

• Focus attention on the fact that Jesus is the light of the world. Each time we light our blessed candles, we remember his presence with us to help us on our journey through life.

• Read a children's version of the presentation of Jesus in the temple (Lk 2:22–40).

❏ REFLECT

The reflection might take the form of a short homily explaining the meaning of the Word and how the candle is a symbol of the presence of God in our midst, lighting our way through life.

❏ BLESSING OF CANDLES

Leader:

God of heaven and earth, source of all light, bless these candles and make them holy.

May we who carry them, remember your presence in our midst.

May we always praise and glorify you.

May we walk in the path of your goodness and come with you one day to the light that shines forever.

We make our prayer through Jesus Christ Our Lord. Amen.

(Sprinkle the candles with holy water).

❏ RESPOND

Prayer of the Faithful (read by children)

(The following may provide a basis for the Prayer of the Faithful. However, you might want to encourage and assist the children in writing their own prayers for the occasion.)

Reader one: We pray for all Christians. May they always walk in the light of the teachings of Jesus. Lord, hear us.

Response: Lord, hear our prayer.

Reader two: We pray for our parents and teachers. May they always show us the way to goodness and truth. Lord, hear us.

Response: Lord, hear our prayer.

Reader three: We pray for all people who experience darkness in their lives. We remember especially those who are suffering, people without peace, and people without love. May they experience comfort, strength, and love from their families and friends. Lord, hear us.

Response: Lord, hear our prayer.

Reader four: We pray for our school. May we truly come to know Jesus, as our God, our leader, and our friend, and may we follow his teachings in all that we do. Lord, hear us.

Response: Lord, hear our prayer.

Candles are then lit and distributed—one to each class—with words such as: "Take these candles as a reminder that Jesus is the Light of the World. When you pray, light them as a symbol of the presence of Jesus in your midst. Remember always to try to follow the teachings of Jesus in your lives."

LENT—A TIME FOR RENEWAL

(A prayer service for older children)

❏   PREPARATION

Place on a prayer table or mat a container with soil ready for planting, some wheat sheaves, the Bible, and a lit candle.

Gather the children around the prayer table or center.

Leader: Lent is a time for us to consider turning to Jesus and his teachings in a new and more committed way. As we gather today to pray, let us consider our willingness to model our lives on the life of Jesus.

❏   GATHERING PRAYER

All: *Jesus, you have called us to follow you from the moment of our baptism until now. As we begin the season of Lent, help us to think about our Christian faith and whether we are living our lives in the best way we can. Send your Holy Spirit into our minds and hearts to guide us and help us as we pray.*

❏   FOCUS

Lent is a time for the dying of selfishness and sin and the rising to a new life of love and generosity in Christ.

Symbol: a grain of wheat (give each child a grain of wheat to hold in his/her hand)

Reading: John 12:24–26

❏   REFLECTION

(A guided meditation on the grain of wheat)

Instruct the children:

Look closely at the grain of wheat in your hand. Consider its size—its smallness as it rests in the palm of your hand.

Feel it between your fingers and notice the hardness of the husk which protects the life within.

Observe its color and its shape.

Let the grain of wheat remain in your open palm and close your eyes for a few minutes to ponder the wonder of this tiny seed.

In your imagination, picture yourself planting your grain of wheat in healthy, fertile soil. See it being watered and placed in a warm, sunny position where it will germinate and bring forth new life.

Imagine you can watch the germination process as it happens. Notice how the hard outer husk is broken—how it splits open to allow the new seed to come to life. See the husk fall away and eventually shrivel and die.

Watch the new seed extend its shoots upward and its roots down into the soil. Picture the green stem growing taller and taller and then forming the sheath that will one day provide bread for our tables and further seed for sowing.

Now enter your heart or special place where you can talk to Jesus. Imagine that you are the seed.

Ask yourself what part of your life is like the hard outer husk. Is there something in your life that prevents you from being truly Christian—that prevents the life of Jesus from bursting forth in you?

Is there a hardness that stops you from loving someone?

Jesus is with you in your heart or special place. He wants you to grow in love and generosity.

If you are able, offer him your grain of wheat and ask him to help you to let go of all hardness, selfishness, and unforgiving and unloving behaviors.

If you can identify an area of your life that you would like to improve, speak to Jesus about this. Tell him that you will make a real effort to change for the better.

Remember, the husk of wheat must be broken open if new life is to emerge. Jesus can give you the courage to take this step.

Allow a few moments of silence. Perhaps play some background music to assist the silent prayer. Then, continue the instruction:

Open your eyes now and look at the grain of wheat in your hand. Remember your conversation with Jesus.

❏   RESPONSE

Action: Have each child place his/her grain of wheat in the previously prepared soil.

The action is a symbol of the dying/giving up of some negative aspect in their lives and the taking on of new attitudes and behaviors which will help them to be more like Jesus.

Place the newly planted seeds in a warm, sunny spot in the classroom. Keep them watered and over the next few days the seeds will begin to sprout.

As the seeds continue to grow throughout the season of Lent, they provide a symbolic reminder to the children of the new life that comes from friendship with Jesus and our will-ingness to follow his way of life.

For each lenten class, gather around the seeds to pray.

Leader: Lord, we know that the promise of life in the wheat
is a promise of new life in us.
If we have the courage to let go of some of the things
that keep us from being fully alive in you,
then Easter this year will have special meaning for us.
We know that you will help us
and rejoice in our attempts to make our lives more like yours.

All: Jesus, you have called us to come and follow you.
Help us to remember during this season of Lent that you are with us always.
Thank you for your presence.
Thank you for your Spirit.
We make this prayer together in your name. Amen.

EASTER: JESUS IS ALIVE; HE IS WITH US

❏   PREPARATION

Prepare a prayer table or mat decorated with flowers. Place on it a paschal candle and a Bible. You may also wish to include a suitable picture of the resurrection and/or a symbol or picture of the empty tomb.

❏   FOCUS

Jesus is alive and is with us.

Leader: Today, we gather to celebrate our belief that Jesus rose from the dead, that he is alive and is with us.

After Jesus rose from the dead, he appeared to his friends a number of times. It was difficult for them to believe that he had risen from the dead. The disciples did not immediately recognize Jesus when he appeared to them because he seemed to be somehow different. He appeared as a gardener, a traveler, and a fisherman.

These gospel stories of Jesus' appearances to his friends help us to realize that Jesus is truly risen from the dead and that he continues to be with us today. The events of Easter challenge us to recognize Jesus in the people around us, in the scriptures, and in the breaking of bread (eucharist).

Read or tell one of the post-resurrection narratives from the gospel of John (chapters 20 and 21) or from Luke (24:13–35).

❏ REFLECTION

Discuss with the children the meaning of the story you have chosen, emphasizing the two aspects: Jesus is alive and Jesus is with us.

❏ RESPONSE

Leader: Jesus, we believe that you rose from the dead.

Response: Jesus is alive. Jesus is with us.

Leader: Jesus, we believe that you are present in the people around us.

Response: Jesus is alive. Jesus is with us.

Leader: Jesus, we believe that we meet you in the Word of the scriptures.

Response: Jesus is alive. Jesus is with us.

Leader: Jesus, we believe that you are present in the bread of the eucharist.

Response: Jesus is alive. Jesus is with us.

Leader: Jesus, sometimes we forget that you are truly alive and present in our world. We forget that you are our God and our friend, that you died for us, and that you love us and want to help us in our journey through life.

Today we ask you to increase our faith and to open our eyes so that we may recognize you in the scriptures, in the eucharist, and in the people we meet.

❏　CONCLUSION

Conclude with an Easter song.

UNIVERSAL CHILDREN'S DAY

❏　PREPARATION

- Have the children complete projects or bring pictures that could become the focus for a prayer service praising God for all children everywhere.

- Place the pictures or projects in a circle around a prayer mat or prayer table.

- Place a lighted candle and a picture Bible on the table or mat. Have the Bible open at a picture of Jesus with children.

- Decorate the table or mat with other suitable objects such as a globe of the world, symbols of other cultures, etc.

- Gather the children in a circle around the prayer mat.

❏　GATHER

Sing a gathering song that is familiar to the children.

❏　FOCUS

Jesus loves all children, everywhere. He wants us to do the same.

Leader:　Today we have gathered together to praise God for all the children of the world, to pray for them, and to show our care for them in a practical way.

　　　　　Matthew, Mark, and Luke all tell us that Jesus loved children, that he welcomed them and blessed them.

　　　　　Let us listen to the story from the gospel of Mark.

❏　SCRIPTURE

Read Mark 10:13–16.

❏　RESPONSE

Leader:　Let us praise and thank God for all children, everywhere.

Response: We praise and thank you, God, for all children, everywhere.

Prayer (led by designated children):

Reader One: God, you are the creator of all children. (Response)

Reader Two: You made children to live in different lands and speak different languages. (Response)

Reader Three: You created children of different abilities, giving to each special gifts and talents to share with others. (Response)

Leader: Let us ask God's forgiveness for not always showing love and appreciation for all God's children.

Response: Lord, have mercy.

Prayer (led by designated children):

Reader Four: For the times when we have laughed at or hurt other children. (Response)

Reader Five: For the times we have unfairly excluded other children from playing or working with us. (Response)

Reader Six: For not bothering to care about children in need. (Response)

Leader: Let us ask God to bless the children of our world.

Response: God bless children, everywhere.

Prayer (led by designated children):

Reader Seven: We ask your blessing, Lord, on children who are well and happy. (Response)

Reader Eight: We ask your blessing, Lord, on children who are sad, those who are hurting, those who are sick, those who are hungry, and those who are dying. (Response)

Reader Nine: We ask your blessing for all the children of all the lands in our world. (Response)

Leader: God our Father, you have created all children to know you and to enjoy the life you have given them. Teach us to care for each other, to help each other live happy and fruitful lives.

We make our prayer through Jesus Christ, Our Lord. Amen.

❏   ACTION

Children may participate in an action of justice, peace, and love, such as:

- writing letters to children in the hospital

- taking up a collection of coins, the proceeds of which could go to a children's charity

- going without food for one meal and contributing the proceeds to a children's charity

- inviting children with special needs to join them for a social activity.

❏   CONCLUSION

Conclude this prayer service with a hymn that focuses on God's love.

❏   NOTE

The format for a prayer service is very simple, but it allows for many different types of prayer.

The prayer service may take anywhere from five minutes to twenty-five, depending on the theme, the occasion, and the age of the children.

Occasionally parents may be invited to participate in the planning and/or the implementation of the service.

It is very important that the prayer be owned by the participants, therefore the above suggestions are just that—suggestions not prescriptions. They are offered as starters for enthusiastic and prayerful teachers and catechists.

PRAYERS FROM OUR HERITAGE

The Catholic Church community has a number of traditional prayers that have been prayed and handed down through the centuries from one generation to the next. These prayers form an integral part of the devotional life of Christians. It is important for the children in our schools and parish programs to be introduced to such prayers so that they are able to participate in the prayer of the community whenever it gathers.

TRADITIONAL PRAYERS

OUR FATHER

*Our Father
who is in heaven,
hallowed be your name.
Your kingdom come;
your will be done
on earth as it is in heaven.
Give us this day our daily bread
and forgive us our trespasses
as we forgive those
who trespass against us.
And lead us not into temptation,
but deliver us from evil.
For yours is the kingdom,
the power and the glory,
now and forever. Amen.*

HAIL MARY

*Hail Mary,
full of grace,
the Lord is with you.
Blessed are you
among women
and blessed is the
fruit of your womb,
Jesus.
Holy Mary,
mother of God,
pray for us sinners
now and at the hour
of our death.
Amen.*

GLORY BE

Glory be to the Father,
and to the Son,
and to the Holy Spirit,
as it was in the beginning
is now, and ever shall be
world without end. Amen.

GRACE BEFORE MEALS

Bless us, Lord,
and these your gifts,
which of your goodness
we are about to
receive, through
Christ, Our Lord.
Amen.

GRACE AFTER MEALS

We give you thanks, almighty God, for all these gifts which we have
received from your goodness, through Christ Our Lord. Amen.

HAIL HOLY QUEEN

Hail, holy Queen,
mother of mercy;
hail our life, our sweetness,
and our hope.
To you do we cry,
poor banished children
of Eve.
To you do we send up our
sighs, mourning, and weeping
in this valley of tears.
Turn then, O most gracious
advocate, your eyes of mercy
towards us, and after this
our exile, show unto us the
blessed fruit of your womb,
Jesus.
O clement, O loving,
O sweet Virgin Mary.

Pray for us,
O holy mother of God,
that we may be made
worthy of the promises of Christ.
Amen.

THE APOSTLES' CREED

I believe in God, the
Father almighty, creator
of heaven and earth;
and in Jesus Christ,
his only Son, our Lord;
who was conceived by the
Holy Spirit, born of the
Virgin Mary, suffered
under Pontius Pilate, was
crucified, died, and was
buried. He descended to
the dead. On the third
day He rose again from the
dead. He ascended into
heaven and is seated at the
right hand of the Father.
He will come again to judge
the living and the dead.
I believe in the Holy
Spirit, the holy Catholic
Church, the communion of
saints, the forgiveness of
sins, the resurrection of
the body, and life everlasting.
Amen.

ANGELUS

The angel of the Lord declared unto Mary.

Response: *And she conceived by the Holy Spirit.*
Hail Mary...

Behold the handmaid of the Lord.

Response: *May it be done unto me according to your word.*
Hail Mary...

And the word was made flesh.

Response: *And dwelt among us.*
Hail Mary...

Pray for us O holy mother of God.

Response: *That we may be made worthy of the promises of Christ.*
Let us pray:

Pour forth we beseech you, O Lord, your grace into our hearts; that we to whom the incarnation of Christ your Son was made known by the message of an angel, may, by his passion and cross be brought to the glory of his resurrection. Through Christ Our Lord. Amen.

PRAYER FOR PEACE (attributed to St. Francis of Assisi)

Lord, make me an instrument of your peace.
Where there is hatred, let me sow love;
where there is injury, pardon;
where there is doubt, faith;
where there is despair, hope;
where there is darkness, light;
where there is sadness, joy.

O Divine Master, grant that I may not seek so much
to be consoled, as to console;
to be understood, as to understand;
to be loved, as to love.
For it is in giving that we receive;
it is in pardoning that we are pardoned
and it is in dying that we are born to eternal life.

PRAYER TO THE HOLY SPIRIT

Come, Holy Spirit, fill the hearts of your faithful and kindle in them the fire of your love.

Send forth your Spirit and there will be a new creation and you will renew the face of the earth.

Let us pray:

O God, you instruct the hearts of the faithful by the light of the Holy Spirit, grant that by the same Holy Spirit we may ever relish what is right and ever rejoice in his consolation. Through Christ, Our Lord. Amen.

PRAYER FOR THE FAITHFUL DEPARTED

Eternal rest grant unto them, O Lord

Response: *And let perpetual light shine upon them.*

May their souls and the souls of all the faithful departed, through the mercy of God, rest in peace.

Response: *Amen.*

PRAYER TO THE GUARDIAN ANGEL

Angel of God, my guardian dear, to whom God's love entrusts me here, ever this day (night) be at my side, to light and guard, to rule and guide. Amen.

A SHORT ACT OF FAITH, HOPE AND CHARITY

My God,

I believe in you,

I trust in you,

I hope in your promises, and

I love you.

PRAYERS FROM OTHER CULTURES AND TRADITIONS

A rich diversity of prayer practices and prayers can be found among the many ethnic and national groups that comprise the Christian Church. Similarly, the prayers of other religious groups in our society can contribute to a greater knowledge about prayer and its practice across all religious traditions.

The home and family prayer practices of students can be a valuable resource for sharing the prayers of different cultural and religious groups. Such sharing helps to develop tolerance and respect for the beliefs and traditions of others.

Take time to look at curriculum texts for examples of prayers from other cultures and religious traditions, and be sure to check your local library for prayer resources.

Of Related Interest ...

Children, Imagination and Prayer
Creative Techniques
for Middle Grade Students
Pat Egan Dexter

The author gives step-by-step directions for bringing students to a new and meditative experience of prayer.
0-89622-565-8, 80 pp, $7.95 (order C-70)

Dear Jesus, Dear Child
Guided Meditations for Young Children
Deborah Roslak and Linda Orber

Joys, fears and needs of primary-grade children are focused on here in an easy-to-use and inviting format.
0-89622-508-9, 96 pp, $9.95 (order B-36)

Leading Students Into Prayer
Ideas and Suggestions from A to Z
Kathleen Glavich

The author explores the varied forms that prayer takes: personal and communal, vocal and mental, liturgical, Scripture-based, centering, and traditional.
0-89622-549-6, 160 pp, $12.95 (order W-68)

Prayers, Activities, Celebrations (and more) for Catholic Families
Bridget Mary Meehan

Encourages families to come together for exercises and activities that reinforce their faith, strengthen family ties and solidify Catholic values.
0-89622-641-7, 72 pp, $7.95 (order M-38)

Family Prayer for Family Times
Kathleen O'Connell Chesto

This book emphasizes the importance of establishing and maintaining prayer traditions in the home. It offers general guidelines, as well as specific examples and complete prayer rituals.
0-89622-668-9, 144 pp, $9.95 (order M-53)

Available at religious bookstores or from:

TWENTY-THIRD PUBLICATIONS
XXIII P.O. Box 180 • Mystic, CT 06355 • 1-800-321-0411